Orange Butterfly

OctobeRaine

Copyright © 2014 OctobeRaine
Cover: Reem Debs
Muse: Alice's Lover
Encouragement: MOJ
All rights reserved.

ISBN: 1499159056
ISBN 13: 9781499159059

The truly liberated are the ones who conquer their fear of pain and choose to fall in love.

Come, let us fall in love...

Suddenly

Till that moment
I didn't realize
My soul had stopped breathing
Waiting for this very moment
Till that moment
I didn't know
My heart was barely beating
Waiting for that moment
Till that moment
I didn't feel
My body was not alive
Waiting for that moment

Suddenly
There you were
Standing just there

My soul starts to breathe
Small, shallow, quick breaths
My heart starts to beat
A hard, pounding beat
My body comes alive
So sensitive, so aware
That finally
You are here

Suddenly
The world stops turning
And starts in a new direction
And everything is crumbling
Bowing to this new violation
It's all falling apart
The old order

Suddenly
I come alive

Falling

In the deepest of the darkest night of my soul
I meet you
A journey that I want to take
Without fear
Without thinking
Without shame
I give you everything
My broken heart
My mixed-up head
My cold, cold body

You are the fire, and I am the moth
I will fly into you
My weakness, my pain, my sorrow
All reflected in the heart of your flame
I see my fights, my triumphs, my remaining tomorrows
All illuminated in your light.

Your light
It surrounds me, engulfs me in its incandescence
Closer
Deeper
Swiftly
I fall into you
I choose to exist from inside of you

There are no words
For this thing that has happened, that is happening
I lose my grip on this present reality
In exchange for this sweet, sweet deep insanity
That you are burning right into my heart
I burn without dying
Our flame keeps climbing higher, burning hotter
Fuelled by the many moments that
Were long waiting for this time

In this place there is no reason
There is no need for reason

Lost in you

I lose myself in you
without a thought for me
pain starts to creep up steadily
keeping step with my heartbeat
I love you and no, there's no stopping me
I've lost myself completely in you

I search for the words
but there are no words created that can totally relate
this longing, this craving
this wanting, this needing
this emotional barter
my heart for your heart

My lips have learned to speak
in a way only your body can understand
a beautiful cycle of constant little deaths
high peaks of pleasure
heated thrusts of deep surrender
a joy so exquisite it hurts as it spirals
leaving pools of pure nectar in great measure

I seek distance from you
and spaceless embrace all at once
I want you gone
and want you inside of me all at once

I want to never have known you
and want to be the first and only one to have known you
all at once
I want to be the last
and I want to have been the first
all at once

And here I am
There is me. There is no you.
My Judas heart
lost inside of you

I Love You

I Love You

Something Seriously Crazy

Absolutely. Deeply. Truly.

Always & Forever

8

Qadar

I have fallen into you
Right to the core of you
There are no words for this
That has happened
We don't need them
Like it was
In the beginning
We shall speak
In the ancient tongue
With our minds
Our hearts
Our lips
Our hands
Our bodies

Still you fight me

For every one of your incarnations
I will give you one of mine
Till there's nothing left
But you and me
Then you will understand
What I now know
I am the lesson you have to learn

One day
You will look at me
And it will be clear
You will see
This for what it is

And in that moment
When we touch
It will be like nothing
We ever felt before
A gentleness that begets such utter violence
A completion that begets a new beginning
Time will stop
It will move fast
It will be our past, our present, our future
It won't matter
We will measure our life
In moments
As you and as me
Truth and love
Faith and life
As it was in the beginning

Let's Fall

'Not you'

you said

with your beguiling ways, your seductive self

'Not you'

you said

with your deep, intense eyes, your captivating laugh

'Not you'

you said

with your enticing scent, your sweet, erotic taste

Yes, me, Lover. Me

Look at me

see yourself reflected in my eyes

deep inside of me

Yes, me

who distracts you with my crazy laugh and deep kisses

while I unwrap your heart and set free your mind,

You thought this was it, yourself contained within

even as I pour more of myself, deep into you

you are greedy for every bit of me

for in my presence you know this is part of you

the part that helps you see

far beyond to what could be

You are scared

my naked soul assaults your senses

threatening the barriers that hold your heart within

I am not afraid

to hurt even as I push

hard against the ice, the stone

the flesh, your bone

my wrong for your right

your yes for my no

your heart for my heart

our tears, our blood

our fears, our love

Your need for me

is a slow, growing addiction

leaving trails that burn

first your ego

now your heart

A longing so primitive,

a rhythm so native to us

It hurts

a little and then a lot more

it's never simple

this path that we have chosen

I came to take you to the edge

You are here to carry us over the edge

let's fall. Let's open our eyes and fall

let's be entangled as we fall

let's kiss. Let's fall

I want you

I want you
I want your heart unmasked
No games
No lies
No pretending
No withholding
I want you
Addicted
Obsessed
Unremorseful
Fearless
I want you
This is how I want you

Orange Butterfly

Tears are the words
That my sorrow speaks
Sparkling streams of pain
pouring out of me

Trapped
In this cage
My spirit dies slowly

It seeks light,
love,
laughter
It implodes in on itself
Even as the pain grows bigger
And bigger
Seeking regeneration in another place
Another time
Far
far away from you

You are like poison
Seeping in, smothering
Infecting me with nothingness
This is what I morph into

An orange butterfly
With no wings
to fly

So I wait
I wait
I wait for time to stop
To remember me
A tiny part of this eternity
To reinstate me
To free me from this cruel cycle
of pain
to lead me into the light
to love
to laughter
My wings

Up
up I go
My voice returns
She screams in delight
Unknown words that speak in light

Breathless

Fate whispered
time moved
in the deep darkness of my night
you came to me
I see you
but without this face
our souls speak
of a time past
a memory hidden
now rising, unbidden

We talk
words that fail to capture
the power of our thoughts
we let our passion flow
our tongues intertwined
bodies locking
in an ancient dance
so violent, so heated
a deep melding
making complete
you and me

Looking into your eyes
I see the image of me
powerful and beautiful

burned deep inside of you
I feel the fury of your passion
as it engulfs me completely
burning away all memory of lovers past
till you're all that I see
all that I feel
all that I need

breathless

I run into the safety of me
before you
the emptiness that is safe
free from this madness
that pulls me deeper and deeper
into you

I give in and return to you
walls of ice
deep pools of raging fury
shackles of fear
keep me from reaching you
helpless I cry out
bitter tears
spring from the absolute brokenness within

breathless

I quietly rage at you
barbed words
slicing at your hardened heart
yet you stand unmoved

silence

Fate whispers
time stills
we are in that place
the beginning
I know you
but without this face
we share a secret so ancient, so true
that mere mortal minds cannot behold
love is not peaceful
it is passionate, deep sadness,
extreme joy, pure agony
you fall and fall
from light into darkness
losing your mind, your reasoning
losing your self
it is fire, it is ice
hurting and soothing
an alchemy
that turns us into mortals
of a higher bidding
for we have tasted the fire
of the world
and live

breathless

I wait
a heartbeat
a day
a week
yet you remain unmoved
choosing the safety of life
over the madness in your soul
yet I see

through your eyes
for I am deep inside of you
your world is colored
the blazing red of pain
our passion cannot be contained
now it has tasted the goodness of life
it will die slowly
taking all that is good in you
deep into its flaming vortex
all that will be left
will be the shadow of you
broken and aching

breathless

Fate whispers
time moves
I go
in another time and place
all that will be
will be

Deception

You never should have let me in
never should have fallen for me
you don't let in the light
then run around pulling down the blinds

I am there inside of you
my love runs deep
dangerously entwining your heart with mine

your lips say no
you want me to go
your eyes search mine
looking for what only I know

you used your words to cut me deep
taking away all
that was once mine to keep
you've told your mind a lie
your heart is turned to stone
I am that diamond
that will cut through to your bone

you never should have tasted my love
never should have kept my words
you should never have breathed my air
should never have kept the memory of my smell

you lie
when you say I'm nothing to you
you lie
when you kiss those other girls
you lie
when you stay away from me
you lie
when you try to kill the memory of me

I am the wind that stirs your heart
the heat that warms your flesh
the madness inside your head
the joy that makes you cry

My words are the water you need to grow
and I am the pain you need to know
I am the fire that burns within
the mirror you see a reflection of your soul in

I wait
tomorrow is today
your walls will fall, come what may
I wait
your heart must thaw with pain
you will call my name, again

Tonight

Tonight

In the pub lit by firelight

We sit. Fingers intertwined. We talk

Moments like this

fuelled by kiss after kiss

We smile. My cheek moving up and down your stubble. We sigh

You ask me if I miss you

I miss you.

I miss you in a way that hurts deep, right to the depths of my soul

I ask you to hold time still for us

command the night to wait

while we make love

within a threatening storm

Five minutes. One hour. Three days

will never be enough

The more of us we have, the more of us we want

We stop. We have to because we know.

If we didn't, we would never

and yet, we stop

Every time we part

you say good-bye like it is for the very last time

I kiss you like it is the very first time

We hold each other for a very long time

yet part we must.

tomorrow is a long time coming

346 days and still counting

Remember

In the end
there was just you and I
and so much space
in between us

We have talked
we have fought
we have cried
we have stopped

Silently
we sit and remember
the journey we took
that brought us here
this dark place
filled with dark despair

Fear so thick
it threatens to choke
the little spark left
that glimmers bravely
waiting to lead us
back to life
our life

Silence so loud
it echoes through
holes in us
left by our raging selves
so loud
we can hardly think

It is cold
this emptiness
where our fire once burnt
there's just this empty space
our dreams turned to ash
leaving behind a nasty taste

Fall in Love Slowly

This time

I want to fall in love with you

very slowly

I want to remember your every nuance

recall each and every turn

I want to slow down time

capture the very scent of you

when we start to kiss

when we kiss

My whole being is infused

with the very essence of you

when you breathe me

and I breathe you

when we kiss

I want to remember our rhythm

Remember the way you feel

when you're deep within

this unorchestrated dance

to the wild beating of our hearts

the swift rushing of blood to my head

as I break into words

of pure ecstasy

your drops of sweat

mixing with my tears

I want to slowly etch every inch of you

in my mind

my fingers touching, feeling

revealing the things my eyes cannot see

icy front as hard as diamonds

burning furiously without melting

the slight tremor when we touch

the crazy tattoo of your pulse

I want to remember the deep longing

in your eyes

as you search my face

I want our memories of our time

to be seamless, unending

because even when we sleep

we continue in our dreams

And This Is Me

I am fire
Burning without restraint
Hotter, higher
Devouring, engulfing all with pain

I am wind
Rushing through
Lifting, swirling
A quiet noise, a piercing whistle

Light
Darkness
Noise
Silence

My eyes reflect
The echo
Of my grieving soul

Black
Fiery orange
Midnight blue
Blood-red hue

I am ash
Burning, floating
Up
Up

I am nothing

Beautiful Dream

Part 1

I heed your voice as it calls to me
It's in my head
Softly whispering
'Come'
I rush out into the dark night
Donning its blackness like a cloak
As I run in search of you

I let my heart lead me
Surely I have taken leave of my senses
Your name I do not know
Your face is a bleary haze
When I find you, I will know
Just like that
I will know

I search the faces of strangers
As I run by
But no, none of them is you
The worry, despair, sadness that is life
Deeply etched into their faces
Obscuring their features
So they all look alike

I slow my pace and stop
Panic rising deep within me
Is it possible you are one of them
One in this sea of faceless people
How then will I recognise you?
Helpless, I start to cry

I hear you
So close yet so far away
'Come, I am still waiting'
I kick off my shoes
And raise my skirts
As I race down the emptying streets

Your voice I hear in my waking moments
Your voice I hear in my dreams
Whispering to me ever so softly
I laugh out loud
You are here
I will not doubt
You are here

From afar I hear cars skidding
People screaming obscenities at me
As I cause havoc with my crazy ballet
Across the streets
Down the sidewalks
Streaking across the field
Searching for you

Surely fate isn't so cruel
That I won't find you
Before light,
Before long,
Before years to come

Beautiful Dream

Part 2

The moon is full and red
I find myself in the middle of a shantytown
I slow to a walk
Surely you are not here
This place that reeks of hopelessness
And broken dreams

I look around and see a brightly lit spot
Down the street
I move towards it
Like in a trance
I realise
I can no longer hear your voice

The music comes to me faintly
Some tune I don't recognise
Why?
Why am I following a dream
For it is what you are
Nothing but a beautiful dream

Only in my dreams do you come to me
Your eyes laughing, mocking
My lack of knowing

You are silent
As you strip me
Slowly
Holding me captive with your eyes
As you start to touch me

I am so caught up in you
I cannot move
So confused
I don't try to stop you

Why are you
A complete stranger
Doing this to me
You laugh quietly
And I see the answers there
In your eyes
'This is what you want, what you always longed for
Freedom to be, to lose yourself in this sweet, sweet insanity'
And then you are gone

Beautiful Dream

Part 3

I see you at the corner
Leaning against a pillar
Waiting for me
I am afraid to breathe
As I walk quickly towards you
Lest you disappear into the mists
Swirling around us
I fear your presence is a mirage
For my thirsting soul
An illusion, in my near-demented mind
With every step
I ask myself
Why I have allowed myself to succumb
To your surreal seduction
I might be crazy but I know
That this that I feel
That you have woken up in me
Is no lie, it's very real
Love is too weak a word
To capture the depth of my desire
It cannot explain
How I know you
Without actually meeting you
Or why my body burns

Just thinking of you
I snap back to the present
To meet your absence
I touch the wall where you were
I knew you wouldn't be there
I hear you laugh ever so faintly
And your voice within me
Whisper ever so softly
'Soon, my darling, soon'

I Miss You

Short Version: I Miss You

Longer Version: I Miss You Something Seriously Crazy

Full Version: The only time I don't miss you is when we are in the same space, breathing the same air

Orange Butterfly II

You fell in love with
My face, my laugh
My voice, my touch
But that is only a part of me
You struggled with
My cutting tongue, my distance
My complexities, my cold core
But that is only a part of me
You love me
But I make you hate me
You want me
But I make you fight me
You need me
But I make you want to kill me
But that is only a part of me
I love you
I am in love with you
I am in lust with you
I am lost in you
And that is everything that is true of me

And this is what love is

Love indeed is a form of madness.

Indiscriminate in its choosing
Unconditional in its giving
Unbridled in its growing
Unremorseful in its failing

Love is infinite
Without limits
Without boundaries
Unafraid to go where the heart leads
Even as the mind stumbles and resists

Love doesn't stop
Because you don't believe it
It fights quietly
It fights violently
It fights for the right to be

Love doesn't understand "impossible"
Finds a way round every obstacle
Will walk through fire
Will bear great pain

Total surrender
That is what love is.

Printed in Great Britain
by Amazon.co.uk, Ltd.,
Marston Gate.